THE GALE & POLDEN TRAINING SERIES

THE FIGHTING PATROL

By

COLONEL G. A. WADE, M.C.

AUTHOR OF
" The Defence of Bloodford Village," etc.

*This book should be read
in conjunction with*
" FIGHTING PATROL TACTICS "
" FIGHTING PATROL TRAINING "

The Naval & Military Press Ltd

Published by

The Naval & Military Press Ltd

Unit 5 Riverside, Brambleside
Bellbrook Industrial Estate
Uckfield, East Sussex
TN22 1QQ England

Tel: +44 (0)1825 749494

www.naval-military-press.com
www.nmarchive.com

SUMMARY

HOME GUARD DEFENCE.

TYPES OF PATROL.

    Standing Patrol—keeps tactical point under **observation.**
    Reconnoitring Patrol—obtains **information.**
    Fighting Patrol—observes, **fights,** reports and plays hell
        generally.

EXHILARATING ADVENTURE.

    Crusading spirit.
    First response to **invader.**
    Honour to be selected.

OBJECTS OF FIGHTING PATROL.

    (1) To protect **Main Body** against **surprise.**
    (2) To attack **Small Bodies** of enemy.
    (3) To harass **Large Bodies** and **stop assembly** for attack.
    (4) To prevent **enemy reconnoitring** our positions.
    (5) To dominate **No Man's Land.**

DEFINITE TASK.

    Marked by **clear-cut boundaries.**

STRENGTH.

    Day.—Three Sections of 8 and Leader.
    Night.—Eight only.

EQUIPMENT.

    Mobility.
    No **flash**—no rattles.
    L.M.G. very useful.

FORMATION.

    For **All-round Defence.**
    Depends on concealment, control, protection **and ground.**
    Closer formation by **night.**

MOVEMENT.

    Importance.
    Bounds.
    Quick in **open**; deliberate in **shadow** or **cover.**
    Line of approach—choose carefully.
    Avoid **open spaces.** Keep in **shadows.**
    Danger of **recurring movement.**
    Men should "**freeze**" at end of bound.
    Ambushes. Look out for them.

UNEXPECTED ACTION.
(Give examples, Plate 4.)

DO NOT RETURN BY SAME ROUTE.
(Give examples, Plate 5.)

KEEP OFF SKYLINE.

AVOID CRACKLY TWIGS, ETC.

DO NOT ALARM BIRDS.

COMMUNICATIONS.
Non-human sounds.
Signals to be passed by patrol: —
"Advance," "Retire," "All clear," "Danger," "Prepare to attack," "Attack," "Lost touch," "Enemy," "Right," "Left," "Rear," "Front."

Field signals.

GENERAL OBSERVATIONS.
Coughs.
Stones.
Quiet—Beware!
Do not crawl too soon.
Wrist watches.
Trip wires.
Traverse open ground early.
Do not leave tracks.
Bicycles.
Hostile aircraft.

CONCLUSION.
Scouts.
Do not use more than necessary.
General fault—scouts too close.
No protection unless well out.

Slowness.
Besetting sin of fighting patrols.
Modern warfare accelerated.
To obtain speed, risks must be taken.
Greatest risk is to be overcautious.

Do not take lecture too literally. Use your common sense.
Apply general principles.

Leadership. The decisive factor.

Next Lecture.

>Fighting patrols under invasion conditions.
>Examples of good leadership.
>Inspire you to do likewise.

Practise between now and next lecture.

ENDING.

>There is a lot to be learnt and we may not have much time, so set about it; for, believe me, it is WELL WORTH LEARNING.

THE FIGHTING PATROL

BEFORE we discuss fighting patrols in detail it is essential that you should have a clear picture in your mind of the way in which they would, under invasion conditions, fit in with the general scheme of defence.

The countryside will be divided into centres of resistance, all more or less closely interlinked.

Towns and villages will be defended by all-round defensive posts situated at tactical points and mutually supporting.

Somewhere near the centre of these will be a KEEP, which will be very strong and capable of being held against a considerable force.

The defensive posts and the keep will not only hold men for their own defence, but will contain mobile detachments ready to sally forth and smite any enemy located within hitting distance.

Now in order to make men available for manning these posts, and for the mobile parties, it is necessary to do away with all odd posts and detachments and to concentrate all available personnel.

As a consequence there may be considerable areas between the centres of resistance without posts or static defence of any kind.

To cover these areas will be largely the work of the fighting patrols, who will systematically and regularly cover the country round their defensive posts; always on the prowl, stealthily and quietly, always looking out, always ready to attack any intruder. In this way the enemy is prevented from surprising the main defences, from sending forward patrols or scouts to get information about the defending forces, and is constantly harassed and hindered.

It simply means that small bodies of the enemy (such as parachutists) will never succeed in getting anywhere near the main defence positions, but will be attacked and scuppered in the forward areas by the fighting patrols.

PLATE 1

KEEP

DEFENSIVE POST

Plate 1 shows a typical arrangement of defences of two villages and the countryside by neighbouring units.

You will observe the defence of two localities together with the position of their respective keeps, and all round the localities the areas covered by their fighting patrols.

The patrol areas are bounded by natural features wherever possible; if not, by lanes, ditches or hedges, so that there is not much danger of patrols wandering off in mist or darkness and coming into conflict with neighbouring patrols. In the case illustrated, the main road forms a common meeting place between patrols from each locality.

Although only two defended areas are shown, others would probably come very close.

Patrols are of three kinds—Standing, Reconnoitring and Fighting.

The STANDING PATROL is a small party of men under an N.C.O. placed well in advance of main position to watch the enemy, his line of approach or a place where he could concentrate.

The difference between a standing patrol and a defensive post is that the patrol may have orders to withdraw in face of an enemy advance, but a defensive post holds out to the bitter end.

A RECONNOITRING PATROL is used to obtain special information, to give warning of the enemy's approach, and to secure the main body against surprise.

It has been laid down that "No hard-and-fast line can be drawn between the duties of reconnoitring and fighting patrols." The former usually try to do their job without coming into conflict with the enemy, while the latter are stronger and may have assigned to them the task of countering enemy patrols, destroying parachutists, and generally harassing the enemy. It is this latter type of patrol which we are now discussing.

Having a clear grasp of the function of the fighting patrol in the main scheme of things, we can begin a detailed study of its tactics, but before doing so let us consider for a moment what a splendid thing a fighting patrol is, what a wonderful unit to command, and what an extraordinarily exhilarating adventure to take part in.

It is typical of the crusading spirit which has built up the Empire and kept it safe.

Let us make it the first buoyant, bold and deadly response to any invader who has the bloody impudence to set foot on British soil.

A man selected for fighting-patrol duties may well be proud, and, what is more, once he has mastered fighting-patrol tactics he has learnt the secret of success, no matter whether it is for platoons, companies, battalions or even NATIONS at war.

OBJECT OF FIGHTING PATROLS

(1) To secure main defence line against surprise attack by giving timely warning of the presence of the enemy.

(2) To attack and destroy parachutists and small bodies of the enemy and to hinder and harass larger bodies, giving them no opportunity to reconnoitre our positions or assemble for attack.

(3) Should the enemy be held up, to maintain complete domination of No Man's Land.

Before setting out the fighting patrol will always have very clear and definite orders given to it, defining its task and limiting its sphere of operations.

STRENGTH OF FIGHTING PATROLS

This will, of course, vary considerably owing to local conditions, but for normal purposes by day a patrol of about twenty to twenty-five strong divided into three sections will be the ideal.

It is small enough to be easily under control of its Leader, and yet it is large enough to attack fair-sized parties of the enemy.

By night difficulties of control, combined with the vital need for quietness, render it advisable to split the day patrol into three night patrols.

EQUIPMENT

Mobility is of great importance, and equipment should be as light as possible, just rifle, bayonet and S.A.A. (the last-mentioned carried in pockets), and a few bombs and " Molotovs."

The Leader should have revolver or tommy-gun, compass and field-glasses.

Nothing bright likely to flash in the sunlight or moonlight should be worn, and all equipment should be tested to see that there are no rattles anywhere; if necessary, bits of cloth should be tied round rifles or scabbards.

A Browning rifle or L.M.G. is very useful on patrol to give covering fire or ambush the enemy.

TACTICS—FORMATION

NEVER FORGET, the fighting patrol, like all other detachments of troops, is responsible for its own protection ALL ROUND; consequently, it adopts a formation which will protect it from surprise attack coming from *any* direction.

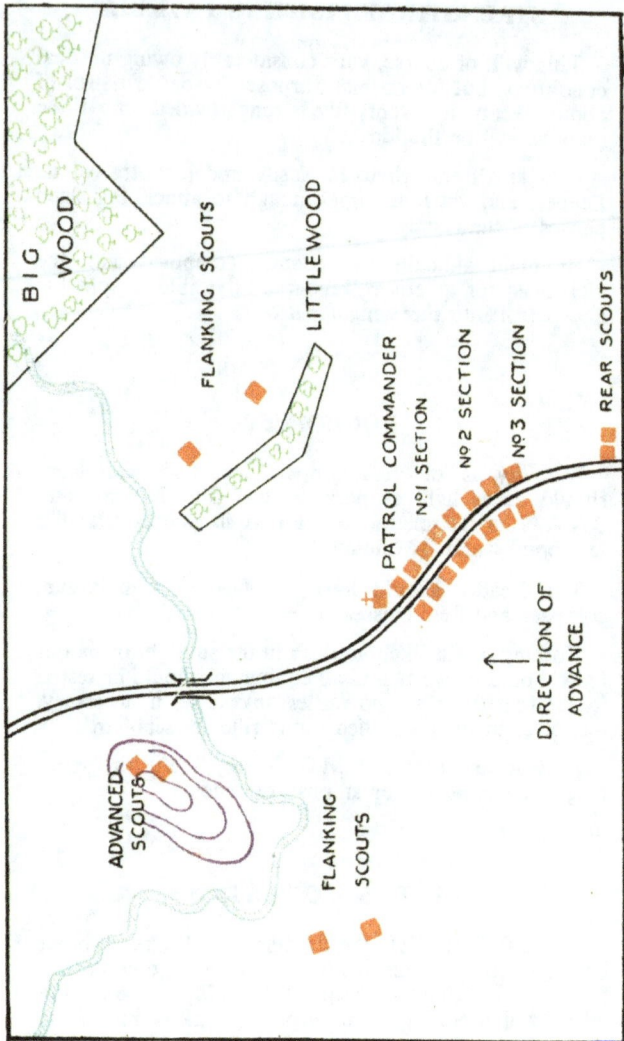

BIG WOOD

FLANKING SCOUTS

LITTLEWOOD

PATROL COMMANDER
Nº1 SECTION
Nº2 SECTION
Nº3 SECTION

REAR SCOUTS

DIRECTION OF ADVANCE

ADVANCED SCOUTS

FLANKING SCOUTS

PLATE 2

Fighting Patrol Advancing in Proximity to Enemy

The two advanced scouts are studying the country ahead from the hill. The right flanking scouts are guarding against any attack launched from BIG WOOD under cover of LITTLE WOOD. The left flanking scouts are watching the country behind the hill which cannot be seen by the patrol.

Note the rear scouts.

The Commander may be at the head of the main body or with leading section or in central position. His position should be known to all the patrol.

An equal number of scouts come from each section. The distance of the main body from the screen of scouts will vary very considerably according to nature of ground and visibility. This is an excellent formation for dealing with parachutists, as it covers a good stretch of country. Every wood, piece of dead ground, house or any possible cover for an enemy must be traversed by the scouts, and it must be a POINT OF HONOUR never to allow an enemy to be overlooked by the screen.

On a clear, bright day, in open country, the scouts may be 200 yards or even 400 yards away from the patrol. In fog or darkness they may be only fifty yards away. Generally speaking, scouts should keep AS FAR OUT AS POSSIBLE without losing touch.

This formation will depend on concealment, control, protection and ground.

For purpose of control, the patrol will be kept as COMPACT as possible, but dispositions should always be such that sudden fire from any quarter will pin down only the minimum number.

Usually the patrol will be preceded by scouts and followed by one or two men at a safe distance in the rear.

If the ground is close, scouts should also move on the flanks of the patrol.

By NIGHT formations will be much closer than by DAY, otherwise members of the patrol will lose touch.

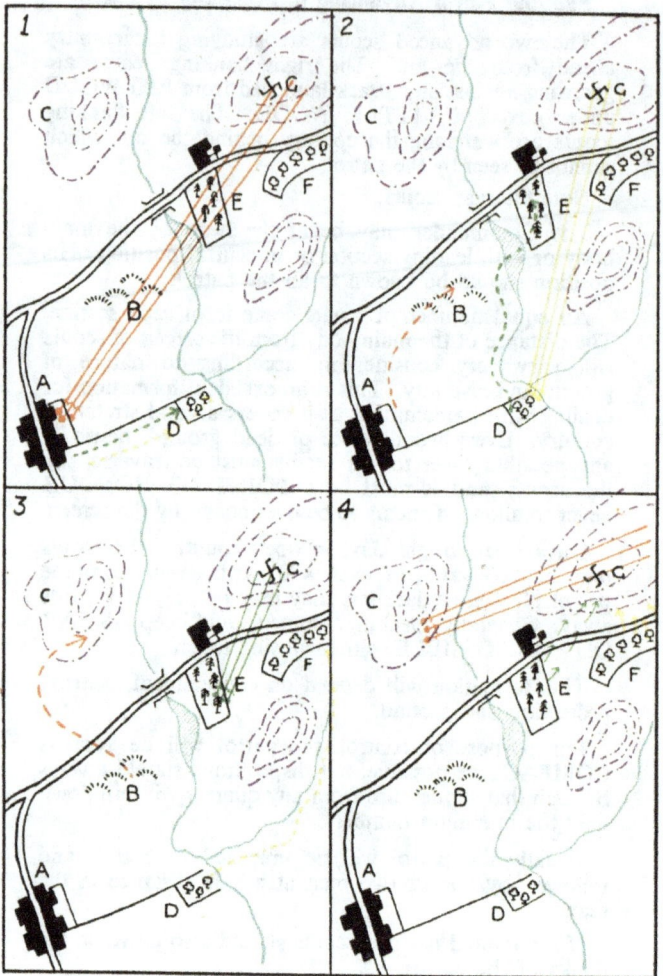

PLATE 3

12

TACTICS—MOVEMENT

To move properly is the fighting patrol's most important requirement. In daylight a patrol will usually move by bounds, and careful study by the Leader is essential to safe and successful progress.

Before making each bound the Leader will carefully select the route to be taken and the spot where the bound will end.

Progress should be quick over spaces where there is a strong light and little or no cover, and deliberate in the shadows or where there is good protection from view.

Fighting Patrol Advancing under Enemy Fire
(PLATE 3.)

Enemy opens fire from HILL G as patrol leaves edge of VILLAGE A. Patrol Leader decides to ATTACK.

First Step.—No. 1 Section opens fire from A while Nos. 2 and 3 Sections proceed to cover at D.

Second Step.—No. 2 Section gives covering fire from D while No. 3 Section goes to WOOD E and No. 1 Section to hollow at B.

Third Step.—No. 3 Section fires from edge of WOOD E while No. 1 Section gains protection of HILL C and No. 2 Section goes along bed of STREAM to WOOD F.

Fourth Step.—No. 1 Section gives heavy covering fire while Nos. 2 and 3 Sections close with enemy.

You see how important ACCURATE, WELL-APPLIED COVERING FIRE is.

Note.—Fire control is most important because if the covering fire is continued too long some of our own men may be shot, and if it ceases too soon enemy can inflict casualties on attacking sections.

In settling upon the next bound do not end it in an obvious place if you can choose one less obvious, even if the latter has not quite such good cover.

Choose your line of approach very carefully, and move on the shadow side of the bushes, hills or trees, avoiding, if possible, places likely to conceal an ambush.

If there is an open space which cannot be avoided and which may be under the enemy's observation, do not attempt to filter the patrol across one at a time, but have a careful look round and then push them across together.

Nothing attracts the attention of a watcher more than RECURRING movement, such as you get if the men go over one after the other.

When the patrol has reached the limit of a bound every man should select his bit of cover and freeze into absolute stillness while the next bound is being studied.

Particular note should be made of covered routes, landmarks, observation points, obstacles and places where an ambush may be lurking.

As the patrol may come under enemy observation without knowing it, it is wise frequently to do the UNEXPECTED THING.

Examples of this are given in Plate 4.

When on the outward journey, it is well for members of a patrol to glance back so as to be familiar with the appearance of landmarks which may be useful on the return journey.

It is not advisable when a patrol is returning to pass over the same route as in the outward journey, because you *may* have been spotted by the enemy, who will lay an ambush for your return.

This is illustrated on Plate 5.

For the same reason, when covering the same ground do not use the identical route twice running.

In selecting the line of advance low ground should be chosen if possible so that the patrol will not be shown up against the sky.

The low ground usually has the advantage of being softer, so that quieter progress can be made.

14

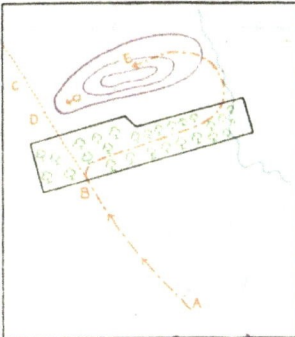

Enemy, having watched patrol move along line A-B, assumes that it will pass through the wood and come out along line B-C, so places L.M.G. to catch the patrol at D.

Patrol, however, changes direction in wood and moves round crest of hill to E, where it sees just below it the expectant Germans gazing at edge of wood. In three minutes latter were never the same again.

When Leader of patrol from A-B reaches A1 he sees movement on crest of hill at C, but instead of stopping he carries right on till he reaches ground enemy cannot see at B; then he goes round the hill to the left and catches enemy (who is eagerly expecting patrol to reappear at D) in the rear, and that is eight Huns less.

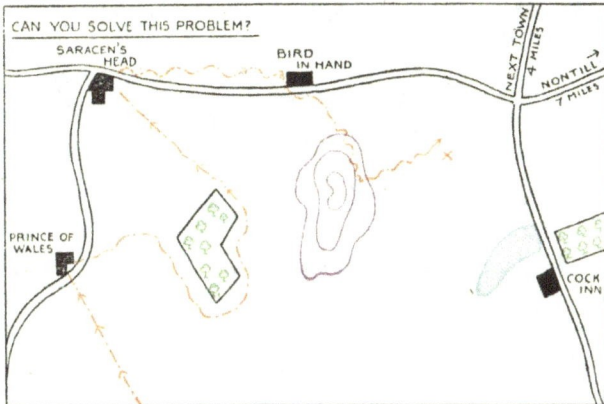

CAN YOU SOLVE THIS PROBLEM?

A patrol of Home Guard have followed course indicated in red and are now at X. Where would you ambush them?

PLATE 4

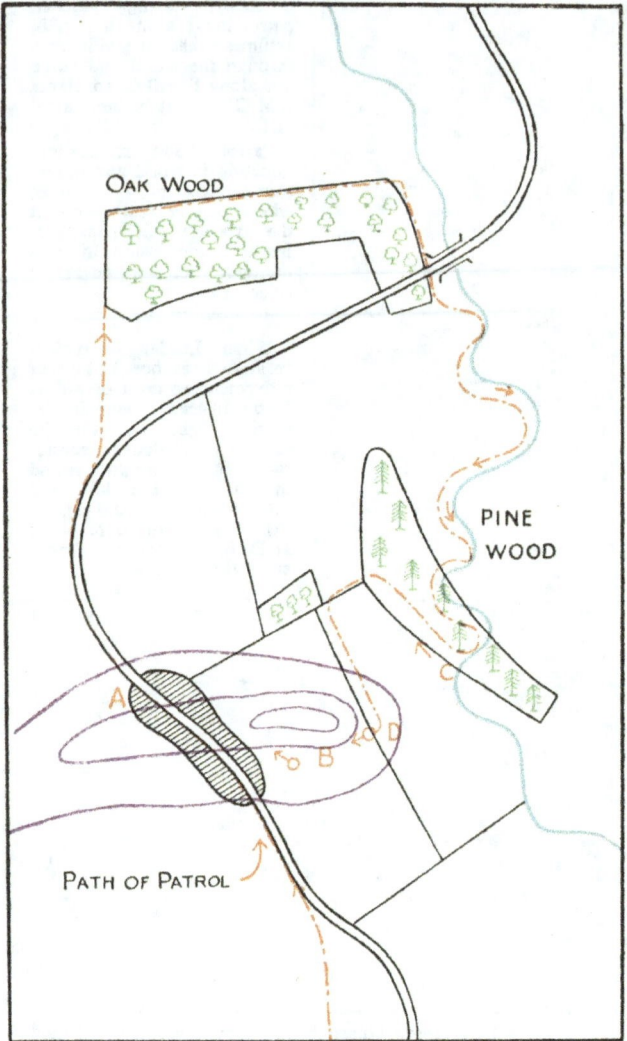

OAK WOOD

PINE WOOD

A

B

C

D

PATH OF PATROL

PLATE 5
16

Advantage of Patrol returning by Different Route

Patrol advancing to reconnoitre OAK WOOD is seen by enemy to pass through sunken road A and in anticipation of patrol's return enemy places machine gun at B. The Patrol Leader, however, decides to return along the stream.

On reaching C, which is the end of a bound, Leader spots the machine gun at B and the patrol makes a detour through the wood, and along the hedge to D, from where they open fire and scupper the lot.

Places where there are crackly twigs should be avoided and care should be taken not to alarm the birds and beasts of the countryside any more than can be helped. Jays and magpies can be a terrible nuisance and will, if disturbed, follow a patrol for hundreds of yards, chattering like a W.V.S. sewing party and alarming the whole countryside.

COMMUNICATION

Communication within the patrol is most important, particularly during darkness, and this can be practised *indoors.*

Where communication is by sounds they should be as little like human sounds as possible. Whispering can carry a long way at night and may give the whole show away, so that sounds which are NON-HUMAN should be the means of communication where members of the patrol cannot touch each other.

Beats on the ground with the palm or the fist will travel a long way, and if done artistically may suggest rabbits to a listening enemy.

It is also possible to convey messages by rubbing pieces of sandpaper together.

A birdlike whistle is passable but not quite so good, and, of course, the romantic thing is the hoot of an owl.

In addition to various recognition signals, a patrol should be capable of passing the following signals, by touch or non-human sounds: —

1. " Advance."	7. " Lost touch."
2. " Retire."	8. " Enemy."
3. " All clear."	9. " Right."
4. " Danger."	10. " Left."
5. " Prepare to attack."	11. " Rear."
6. " Attack."	12. " Front."

All members of the patrol should be well exercised in delivering verbal messages.

On Plate 6 are shown the field signals which should be practised by members of the fighting patrol until every man can make them in a clear-cut, unmistakable manner.

Careful training is required here or the signals may be a source of great danger to the patrol; for instance, if a scout not knowing he is within sight of the enemy makes the signal " Follow me " he may be inviting the patrol to follow him a lot farther than he has in mind.

FIELD SIGNALS

Signals should be made with whichever arm will show most clearly what is meant

In accordance with Infantry Section Leading, 1938

DEPLOY FROM THE CENTRE

DEPLOY TO THE RIGHT

DEPLOY TO THE LEFT

ADVANCE

HALT

RETIRE

CHANGE DIRECTION RIGHT

CHANGE DIRECTION LEFT

RIGHT OR LEFT INCLINE, OR TURN

CLOSE ON THE CENTRE

CLOSE ON THE RIGHT

CLOSE ON THE LEFT

QUICK TIME

DOUBLE

FOLLOW ME

LIE DOWN

AS YOU WERE

ENEMY IN SIGHT IN SMALL NUMBERS

ENEMY IN SIGHT IN LARGE NUMBERS

NO ENEMY IN SIGHT

PLATE 6

(This Plate is a reproduction of Gale & Polden's Instructional Wall Sheet, size 40 by 30; published at 9d)

GENERAL OBSERVATIONS

1. Never take a man with a cough on patrol.

2. A couple of stones in the pocket are sometimes useful at night. One thrown some distance away may distract an enemy's attention at the critical moment.

3. If the enemy is very quiet, beware! You are much safer when he is noisy.

4. Do not crawl till you are obliged to; you will lose a lot of time.

5. Wrist watches should not be worn by men on patrol. They may sparkle by day, and if they are luminous they are dangerous at night.

6. Look out for trip wires. If you have to cut a wire get a man to hold it firmly with both hands and cut in between. He can then lay the ends down quietly. Make sure before cutting a wire that it is not connected to a booby trap or an alarm signal.

7. If open ground has to be traversed take the risk early rather than late, i.e., cross it as far away from the enemy as you can.

8. A patrol should do all it can not to leave tracks behind it.

9. Bicycles are a great help to a fighting patrol in some kinds of country. They are quick and very quiet.

10. Should the patrol have to approach a hostile aircraft which has come down, remember that it bristles with machine guns and may be effecting repairs with a view to taking off again.

Upon coming within close range of the aircraft, all except two men should take cover and prepare to fire on signs of hostility or any attempt to destroy the aeroplane. The remaining men will then advance and order the crew to come forward, away from the aircraft and surrender.

Immediately the crew are apprehended they will be searched for arms and papers, and any nearby cover will be examined to see if other members of the crew are in hiding.

This brings me to the end of the first lecture. You know now the function of fighting patrols within the general scheme of things; you know their composition and their drill. There are, however, one or two things which I would like to underline and emphasize.

Do not use more scouts than you need, because it dissipates your force and is exhausting to the men, but under all circumstances at all times the fighting patrol must be protected against surprise; consequently, there should always be scouts whatever is happening.

The general fault (and it is always useful to know what is usually done wrong so that you can guard against it) is that the scouts draw in too close to the main body. One reason is that the patrol always tends to overtake the scouts, and another is the psychological one that when enemies are about the scouts instinctively dislike being too far away from the support of the main body.

If the scouts are not WELL OUT they are little or no protection to the patrol. In other words, if you make a mistake let it be that the scouts are too far out rather than too near.

The besetting sin of all fighting patrols is SLOW-NESS. You see, nowadays fighting is all done in accelerated tempo, paratroops, mechanized infantry and tanks move across the landscape at a great rate. Any Germans who come here will MOVE RAPIDLY, and unless fighting patrols can do likewise they may never encounter the enemy at all.

To move quickly across country in which an enemy is concealed one has to take risks, but, as I shall show in my next lecture, the risks taken in boldly pushing across country and boldly closing with the enemy are trifling compared with the risks you will run if you are overcautious.

The next point is, do not take what I have said *too literally*. Use your common sense. What I am endeavouring to do is to show you the general principles underlying fighting-patrol activities. Apply these and do not be too hidebound. For instance, in the attack drill try attacking with both Nos. 2 and 3 Sections on the same flank, remembering that the principle is that when suddenly attacked (1) you direct heavy fire upon the enemy, and (2) you attack his flank, flanks or rear. In other words, the principle is that you *must* return his fire and you *must* attack him, but exactly how you carry out the principle is a matter which can only be decided *on the spot*.

Finally, the decisive factor is LEADERSHIP.

A patrol well led will work wonders with practically no casualties. The same patrol badly led will achieve nothing and will be easy meat for the enemy.

How can you develop this power of leadership?

That I will tell you in my next lecture, when we will accompany fighting patrols through many adventures under invasion conditions and you will have presented to you instances of good leadership which will inspire you to do likewise.

In the meantime, between now and my next lecture, organize your patrols, exercise them in moving across the countryside, train your scouts, drill your men in attack and defence, and get ready for the more advanced stages of training.

There is a lot to be learnt and we may not have much time, so set about it; for, believe me, it is well worth learning.

NOTES